ALL-PRO FOOTBALL STARS 1978

JERRY BRONDFIELD

SCHOLASTIC BOOK SERVICES
New York Toronto London Auckland Sydney Tokyo

CONTENTS

ALL-PRO
OFFENSE
1977

WR: **Drew Pearson,** Dallas Cowboys
WR: **Nat Moore,** Miami Dolphins
TE: **Dave Casper,** Oakland Raiders
 T: **Dan Dierdorf,** St. Louis Cardinals
 T: **Art Shell,** Oakland Raiders
 G: **Gene Upshaw,** Oakland Raiders
 G: **Joe DeLamielleure,** Buffalo Bills
 C: **Jim Langer,** Miami Dolphins
 Q: **Bob Griese,** Miami Dolphins
RB: **Walter Payton,** Chicago Bears
RB: **Franco Harris,** Pittsburgh Steelers

Wide Receiver
DREW PEARSON
6-0, 183
DALLAS COWBOYS

When you're a wide receiver in the NFL, the name of the game is "confidence." You have to have confidence that you can run all the pass routes required of you (a lot of them for the wide receiver). You must be confident that you can beat the defensive cornerback with a good fake. You have to have confidence in your hands to grab the ball over either shoulder, out in front of you on a long reach, or on the dead run.

When you have all that it adds up to a receiver like Drew Pearson, an All-Pro for the second straight year, with 46 receptions for 535 yards and 4 TDs.

Nobody seemed to want Drew Pearson when he finished up at Tulsa University in 1973. Tulsa had been run-oriented, and although Pearson was a regular, not too many passes were thrown his way. So, nobody drafted him. Dallas took him on as a free agent.

He didn't have great speed but, as a Cowboy coach said, "He could change direction like an antelope and shift gears into all kinds of change of pace. What he could do was leave a defender flatfooted."

After his second year, when he had more than 1,000 yards on 62 catches, the NFL honored him from then on with double coverage. Even so, he kept sharpening his sense of knowing where the defenders were, and kept on streaking into an open spot. With his great hands, he made all sorts of clutch plays.

"I know where Drew is going to be," says Roger Staubach. "If the defense adjusts to cover that spot, I still know he'll find another spot that's open. It makes a quarterback feel very good."

NAT MOORE
5-9, 180
MIAMI DOLPHINS

He's just a little guy by pro standards but he must have been born to do big things. Nobody in the NFL is "bigger" at catching the ball and then running with it.

A third-round draft choice in 1974, Moore had been a great running back at the University of Florida. He had a way of squirting and darting between and around defenders. But he wasn't afraid of blasting into or over them if he had to. He also was the Gators' prime pass target and in his senior year he had 25 receptions.

"Aha!" said Dolphin coach Don Shula. "A guy who can catch it and run away and hide with it. A wide receiver!" Or words to that effect.

Moore was an instant success. As a rookie he led all Dolphin receivers with 37 catches and 605 yards. Obviously, he was off to stardom. But in 1976 he broke a leg in the ninth game, although he'd already snagged 33 passes for 625 yards and four TDs to lead Dolphin receivers the third straight year. His leg completely healed and last season he was better than ever. With Bob Griese making his remarkable comeback, Moore caught 52 aerials for 765 yards and 12 TDs. The Dolphins just fell short of making the playoffs.

A lot of experts think the Griese-Moore combination is going to explode even more brilliantly this year. How can you improve on perfection? Take a look at the Dolphins next time they're on the tube, and see.

Tight End
DAVE CASPER
6-4, 230
OAKLAND RAIDERS

People have noticed on TV that when
Dave Casper catches a pass for a touch-

6

down, no matter how spectacularly, he does a little routine. No spiking the ball. No fancy dance. No prancing around with arms raised. Casper's routine is to quietly and calmly hand the ball to the official. As though catching a TD pass is what he's supposed to do, so why all the fuss?

But the experts know the job he does. And the former Notre Dame All-America has now made it two years in a row as All-Pro. Who's to say it won't be three ...and more?

"There's just no one better at all phases of his job," says Raider coach John Madden. "If he's just called upon to block, he explodes out of there and knocks his man right out of the play. If the assignment calls for him to block his man first, and then run his pass route, he does it, bang-bang. He hits, releases off his man, and next thing you know he's slipping into the seams of the zone coverage. He gets open as slick as any tight end I've seen."

There's one other thing. Or two. Casper has great hands for the ball. And once he tucks it away he's like a bull elephant. The secondary has to converge on him mighty fast, because it usually takes two to bring him down.

He doesn't have great speed, but he doesn't waste his moves. He knows where he's going at all times and when he and the ball arrive there together, the Raider drive is closer to the goal line—if not over it.

Offensive Tackle
DAN DIERDORF
6-3, 280
ST. LOUIS CARDINALS

"If I had to describe the ideal offensive tackle," said a veteran NFL coach, "I'd do it this way: about 6 feet 3 inches, weighs about 280 pounds, could block a boxcar off a railroad track, and is smart enough and agile enough never to miss an assignment. Then I'd call him Dan Dierdorf."

Well, there's no way to improve on the description. And there's no way to improve on a guy who has now made All-Pro for the third straight season. Want to bet he won't make it four?

Dierdorf, who was All-America at Michigan, is a big reason why Jim Hart, the Cardinals' great quarterback, is usually sacked fewer times by opposing linemen each season than any QB in the league. "It gives me more confidence," says Hart, "and more time to get my passes off, knowing that Dan is out there in front of me, keeping those big ends from getting to me."

Dierdorf is also a tough, durable player who has not missed a game with an injury in the last six years. He has excellent balance and is never out of position when he makes his block. The perfect offensive tackle.

ART SHELL
6-5, 275
OAKLAND RAIDERS

    Art Shell doesn't like to have anything taken away from him, once it's his. He made All-Pro in 1975 but a year later he felt insulted. The experts "forgot" to honor him again. So, last season Shell decided to teach a few people a lesson. He knocked down or brushed aside defensive linemen all over the league map. "I gotta get back what's rightfully mine," was what he seemed to be saying. He got it back, all right!

Shell is another example proving you don't have to come from a big football school to make it big in the pros. Shell, who had the tough job of playing both ways as a tackle — offense and defense — at Maryland Eastern Shore College, made Little All-America as a senior.

There was nothing little about Shell, at 6-5 and 275 pounds. Drafted No. 3 by the Raiders in 1968, he spent two seasons on the specialty teams. But his explosive blocking was too valuable not to be used for full-time duty. In 1970 he became a starter in the Raiders' great offensive line. He was largely responsible for the Raiders setting an NFL record in 1973 of 18 first downs by rushing against St. Louis.

When the Raiders need a yard on those vital third-and-one situations, they usually go over Shell's position. "We have great confidence in Art," says coach John Madden. "If he can't do it with sheer strength, he'll do it with agility or brains. One way or another he gets it done. There just isn't a better offensive tackle in the league."

Unless you lean toward the other All-Pro choice — Dierdorf.

Offensive Guard
GENE UPSHAW
6-5, 255
OAKLAND RAIDERS

"If I wanted to run just one perfect sweep," says one NFL coach, "I'd want Gene Upshaw to be the guard who's leading the interference."

When Upshaw pulls out of the line to trap or lead his backs, he just explodes out of there. By his second step he's at full steam and has a deadly bead on the guy he's supposed to cream.

Upshaw is another of those rare football players good enough to start as a rookie. He was the Raiders' No. 1 draft pick in 1967 after being versatile enough to play three positions at Texas A&I — center, tackle, and end. He also was small college All-America and played in the Senior Bowl and College All-Star games.

Oakland immediately put him at offensive guard, where he's one of the tallest guards in the pro game. Upshaw, at 6-5 and 255 pounds, has the speed to get out in front of his backs on a wide sweep, and has the strength to open holes straight ahead. He made the old American Football League All-Star team three straight years, 1967-68-69, and when the AFL merged schedules with the NFL in 1970 he was voted onto the AFC Conference All-Star team of the NFL.

Upshaw also has excellent leadership qualities. In college he was a member of the Student Council and Biology Honor Society. "He sets a good example for younger players," say his coaches.

Rugged and durable, he has played in 154 regular season games and 19 post-season contests. For five straight years he has been chosen for the Pro Bowl.

Offensive Guard

JOE DeLAMIELLEURE

6-3, 245

BUFFALO BILLS

14

Joe DeLamielleure always gets his man! When he was at Michigan State he majored in criminal justice. "I wish he'd have gone into crime busting instead of football," said an NFL linebacker. "When he comes out to lead interference you can just see that steely glint in his eye as he concentrates on getting his man. And he nearly always does."

A first-round draft choice in 1973, DeLamielleure became an immediate starter for the Bills and made the All-Rookie team. It has taken him only two years to make the jump to All-Pro. But the way he leads interference and drops back for pass protection, everyone agreed he'd make it soon. He'd also a ferocious straight-ahead blocker on running plays. "I love to run behind Joe," O. J. Simpson said when he was with the Bills. "He's the kind of blocker a ballcarrier should remember in his will."

DeLamielleure made the All-Big Ten team in college three times, and topped it off with All-America in his senior year. This is his third straight year as an All-Pro and, barring injury, he should make it four—and five—and six and so on!

Joe has one more distinction going for him. He has one of the toughest names to spell in the entire NFL. If you don't believe it, take another look.

Center
JIM LANGER
6-2, 253
MIAMI DOLPHINS

There are many things in America that
just keep rolling along, and nothing can

be done about it. (1) Old Man River; (2) rock music; (3) Jim Langer being named All-Pro center. This is the fifth straight year for Langer, and who's to say there won't be a sixth? What a workman, say all the league coaches. He snaps the ball with split-second timing, right on his QB's count. He blocks ferociously and quickly. He drops back to pass protect, expertly. He is tireless. Nothing else is needed, except to stay healthy.

Langer has been lucky that way. Either that or he's too tough to be hurt.

Langer, a linebacker at South Dakota State, was a low draft choice with the Cleveland Browns in 1970. He was released on waivers early in the season and picked up by Miami. It was the best waiver pickup the Dolphins ever made. By 1972 he was Miami's starting center.

Langer won the job by making a difficult switch from linebacker. He had to learn to snap the ball and make a quick, blocking charge. Many big linemen, no matter how strong and quick, can't adjust to the center's chores. It gets confusing when a defensive lineman across from him gets a free swat at him just as he snaps the ball. After that the center must still make his block or get back quickly on pass protection.

Within two years after taking over as center for the Dolphins, Jim Langer was All-Pro.

And the end is not in sight.

Quarterback
BOB GRIESE
6-1, 190
MIAMI DOLPHINS

There were a lot of people who never thought Bob Griese would ever return to the form that made him the NFL's top QB four years ago.... The Dolphins' star, who had led them to two straight victories in Super Bowls VII and VIII, had slipped a bit, along with the whole team. Things like that happen. What a lot of fans didn't know was that Griese was also having a problem with his eyesight... and he couldn't adjust to contact lenses.

Last year Griese was fitted with special full spectacles which he wore behind his mask. Whether it was the spectacles or just his desire to prove he was as great as ever, the former Purdue All-America came back to his previous heights. Brilliantly. Behind his pinpoint passing, the Dolphins were one of the surprises of the season and almost made it to the playoffs again.

Once again he stood back coolly in the pocket — scrambling just once in a while — and picked enemy defenses apart. Short, long, and wide outs. The zippy 10-yarder over the middle or the long bomb 50 yards downfield. And all the while there was the Griese magic as he played his now-he-has-it and now-he-doesn't hand-off slickery with his running backs.

It was all-around quarterbacking at its best for the comeback player of the year. Who knows? Maybe this season his talents will take the Dolphins all the way again.

WALTER PAYTON
5-11, 204
CHICAGO BEARS

It was the final game of the 1977 regular season. Walter Payton had already slashed for 1,805 yards rushing. He needed 199 against the New York Giants to break O. J. Simpson's NFL rushing mark of 2,003 yards.

The day of the game was bitterly cold

and the field was covered with icy sleet. Nobody could get any footing. Not even the best runner in football today. Payton got only 47 yards. Earlier in the year he'd broken Simpson's NFL single-game rushing mark with 275 yards against the Vikings on 40 carries. Don't ever bet against him breaking O. J.'s 2,003-yard season mark.

Payton, from Jackson State, had a good break-in year as a rookie in 1975. Not sensational, but he showed the moves that would get him to the top. And in 1976 those moves led the way for the Bears' surprising comeback from the several poor seasons they'd had.

"It isn't just his speed," says one NFL coach, "it's his blinding quickness. A lot of guys can stop on a dime, but how many can be off, full speed, on their first step?"

And a veteran NFL defensive back says: "He seems to come at you from all directions. I swear, he doesn't know himself which way he's going to cut."

His favorite maneuver looks like a broken play. He'll sweep right, see that he's cut off, and will stop and bolt all the way back to the left side. There won't be a blocker with him, but somehow he'll slice free for big yardage.

"The name of the game is confidence," says Payton. "I told them when I came up that I'd make it. Some people didn't listen because I wasn't all that big."

They're listening now, Walter.

Running Back
FRANCO HARRIS
6-3, 225
PITTSBURGH STEELERS

Franco Harris must have figured it was time he got what he deserved: All-Pro recognition. Two or three years in the recent past, he had come close. But always there was someone named O. J. Simpson or

Chuck Foreman or Otis Armstrong to edge him out. But last year there was no way the fans or the experts could leave him off the honor team. His 1,162 yards on 300 carries (11 TDs) don't even begin to prove his all-around value.

And now he joins the legendary Jim Brown and O. J. Simpson as the only players to gain 6,000 yards in their first six seasons. He already holds an NFL mark of 41 attempts in a single game (against Cincinnati in 1976). A big, punishing runner, 25 carries is a poor day's work for him.

The former Penn State star, who was drafted in the first round in 1972, also dishes out a lot of punishment. Few tacklers can take him on one-to-one and bring him down. At best, they hope to slow him down a step until somebody comes to their aid. He breaks more tackles on sheer power and strength than any runner in pro football. And yet he has surprising speed and cutting ability if he needs it. He doesn't seem to need it often. He just lowers his shoulder and lets the dynamite do the job.

His running was a big reason why the Steelers won two straight Super Bowls in 1974-75. In fact, ever since he was AFC rookie of the year in 1972 the Steelers have been in the playoffs every year.

He's at the peak of his powers now. A lot of people are saying he'll power the Steelers back to the Super Bowl again this season.

ALL-PRO DEFENSE 1977

E: **Harvey Martin**, Dallas Cowboys
E: **Lyle Alzado**, Denver Broncos
T: **Cleveland Elam**, San Francisco 49ers
T: **Larry Brooks**, Los Angeles Rams
LB: **Jack Ham**, Pittsburgh Steelers
LB: **Randy Gradishar**, Denver Broncos
LB: **Tom Jackson**, Denver Broncos
CB: **Roger Wehrlie**, St. Louis Cardinals
CB: **Rolland Lawrence**, Atlanta Falcons
FS: **Cliff Harris**, Dallas Cowboys
S: **Charlie Waters**, Dallas Cowboys

Defensive End
HARVEY MARTIN
6-5, 252
DALLAS COWBOYS

Harvey Martin goes to the movies every night. At home. He studies game films of his performance, running them over and

26

over, looking for flaws in his play (very few) and ways to improve his act. It won't take much improving. When he's through watching himself, he studies game films of his next opponent.

Martin is simply the best pass rusher among the NFL's defensive ends. An argument may come from Bronco fans of Lyle Alzado, but it was the Cowboys who whipped the Broncos in the Super Bowl. Right?

The third-round draft pick from East Texas State broke into the lineup as a rookie. By his second season he was solid. Last year the experts agreed there was no way he could be denied All-Pro status.

He has led the Cowboys in quarterback sacks four years in a row. "It's strictly quickness and technique, playing in our Cowboy defense," he says. "I think we have the best coordinated defensive scheme in the business. I'm not giving away any secrets but it allows me to do my thing: combining my speed with 250 pounds of squeeze."

Martin is as effective off the football field as he is on it. He constantly works with youth groups in his native Dallas and does a lot of volunteer work for charities. He's also a popular radio performer with his own daily program called "The Beautiful Harvey Martin Show," starring "The Hard-Hearted Head-Hunter." His football foes would rather not listen, even when they're in town.

Defensive End
LYLE ALZADO
6-3, 260
DENVER BRONCOS

When Lyle Alzado was a 200-pound teenager on Long Island, New York, he worked as a bouncer in his father's tavern. Nobody ever got far out of line when Lyle was on duty. Right then and there some-body could have predicted that he'd become an All-Pro defensive end.

About 60 pounds later, Lyle Alzado was one of the big reasons for the Bronco's sensational surge to the Super Bowl. And he became a strong factor after knee surgery because of an injury on the first play of the 1976 season that put him out that whole year.

"Where do you find a better pass rusher than Alzado?" his coach, Red Miller, demands. Well, not on too many teams. Maybe just one other is as good — his teammate on the All-Pro.

Brute strength, excellent balance, and a pair of hands that swipe aside anything in his path to the quarterback: those are the tools of Alzado's trade. Not to forget quickness and great savvy for reading offensive plays being run at him.

Alzado was drafted out of little Yankton (South Dakota) College, on the fourth round. But nobody around the NFL really expected him to be a headliner. But in 1971, his rookie year, he played in 12 games. In his second season he was a starter. As a regional (Omaha, Neb.) Golden Gloves heavyweight champion a few years earlier, he had to make a choice. Try for a pro career in the ring — or pro football. There are a lot of backs around the NFL who wish Lyle Alzado had gone after Muhammad Ali's crown instead of them.

CLEVELAND ELAM
6-4, 252
SAN FRANCISCO 49ERS

Cedrick Hardman, the 49er defensive end, nudged a sports writer at practice and gestured toward No. 72. "Cleveland Elam — now there's a hoss! Football players just don't gradually get good. You either have it or you haven't — and ol' Cleveland has it!"

Of course Elam isn't so "ol'." He's young by pro stardom standards. Which means Hardman may be wrong. He's already great and could get better. All that strength! All that agility! All that desire for sacking the QB! The 49ers saw it right away after drafting him fourth in 1975. He'd played four positions at Tennessee State: defensive end, defensive tackle, middle and outside linebacker.

The 49ers tried him first at defensive end and he played in all 14 games as a rookie backup. The following season they spotted him at defensive tackle.

It was his natural home. Opposing QBs wished he'd left it. By last season he was one of the league's leading quarterback sackers. By pro standards he's not all that big, but nobody moves him far out of the path he wants to take — usually toward a meeting with the ball carrier.   "Any time a runner gains more than two yards over me," says ol' Cleveland, "I feel I'm a failure." It's not a feeling that comes over him very often.

Defensive Tackle
LARRY BROOKS
6-3, 255
LOS ANGELES RAMS

    Larry Brooks is the quiet, conservative type. He even works in a bank during the off-season. You can't be much quieter and conservative than that. He's also a perfect example of the athlete who goes further than most people expect. Mostly because of great determination.

Brooks was a 14th-round draft choice of the Rams. He'd played for little-known Virginia State. Even without a lot of press clippings he'd shown enough for the Rams to take a chance on him.

For an athlete like Larry Brooks, that's all he wanted. In training camp in 1972, he did things rookies usually don't do. Like smashing running plays aimed at him in the very first scrimmage. Half way through his rookie year he was a starter. Then, bad luck struck. Half way through the 1975 season he had knee surgery. End of the road?

Not for Larry Brooks. He built the knee back up and in 1976 he was chosen for his first Pro Bowl berth. In 1977 he was truly a star.

"He rarely makes a wrong move," says an admiring pro coach. "In other words, you can't beat him by waiting for him to make a mistake. You've got to just old-fashioned overpower him."

Larry Brooks doesn't overpower easily. He has great strength, especially in his upper arms, which enables him to shuck off the blockers. And in the last two years he's been the Rams' leader in sacking the quarterback. They say he doesn't look spectacular. You don't have to when you get the job done, anyway.

Linebacker

JACK HAM

6-1, 225

PITTSBURGH STEELERS

If you took a poll of all NFL coaches, Jack Ham would no doubt be voted the greatest linebacker in football today. This is his fifth straight year as All-Pro. And because of Ham and a few others who come close to him in ability, linebackers have become some of the most glamorous players in the NFL.

Listen to a former All-Pro linebacker tell it like it is. Wayne Walker, who starred for the Detroit Lions and is now a TV sportscaster says: "Linebackers are usually among the most intelligent players on your team. They have to be, to make the many adjustments the position calls for. They have to defend against the run AND the pass and be able to smell out which it's going to be when so many plays start out the same way. Then they've got to have the speed and mental agility to adjust. And all the while, they're taking a beating from blockers who often crack them good while their attention is elsewhere."

That's Jack Ham. Ham was an All-America at Penn State in 1970. The Steelers made him their second draft pick in 1971 and he rewarded them by making the starting lineup as a rookie. He's not big as linebackers go — only 6-1 and 225 pounds — but he makes up for it in intelligence, quickness, and alertness.

RANDY GRADISHAR

6-3, 233
DENVER BRONCOS

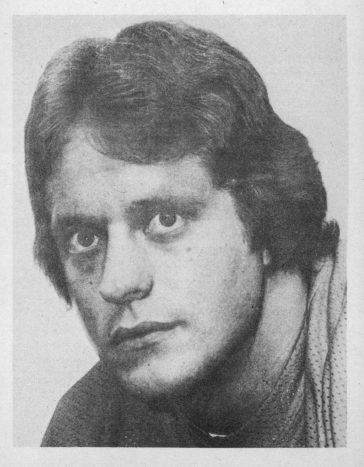

Randy Gradishar plays the middle linebacker spot for the Broncos, which means he has to cover a lot of ground. Anything that comes over the middle or to either side of him is his responsibility. If the outside linebackers get fooled or taken out of the play, the middle man has to cover. With his great speed and zest for the ball, Gradishar seems to be flying all over the place.

He attracted all the pro scouts' attention as an All-America at Ohio State. Woody Hayes, the Buckeyes' famed coach, tagged him as "... the best linebacker I've ever seen." He'd been a three-year starter for the Bucks and an All-America, but the Bronco coaches held their breath a bit. He'd had a complicated knee operation after his final college season and only time would tell if it were successful. Other clubs decided to pass him up. The Broncos gambled and grabbed him on the first round of the 1974 draft.

The knee held up. Gradishar got in a lot of playing time his rookie year and became a starter — and a star — in his second season. He has been the Broncos' leader in tackles the last two seasons. And with his speed and savvy he's a danger-ous defender against the pass. Now that the Broncos have been to one Super Bowl they like the idea. Gradishar provides the kind of rock-ribbed middle defense that could take them there again.

Linebacker
TOM JACKSON
5-11, 220
DENVER BRONCOS

What's that little guy doing out there, playing linebacker for the Broncos? After all, he's only 5-11. Don't worry about it. He plays as though he's eight feet tall.

Tom Jackson is the shortest linebacker in the NFL. A lot of pro scouts thought the Broncos were off their feed when they drafted him on the fourth round in 1973. He'd received a lot of attention as a collegian at Louisville, but nobody seriously thought he'd have a shot at a pro career. Except a couple of Bronco scouts and Jackson himself.

Somehow, it did take him a couple of years to convince the Denver coaches that he belonged in there as a starter. But once they told him the job was his, Tom Jackson took off. He's an exciting player to watch. If there's a faster linebacker in the NFL, the name doesn't come to mind. And because of his speed he's the most effective blitzer the Broncos have. Last year he made life miserable for a lot of NFL quarterbacks. If he didn't actually sack them he certainly hurried them into throwing too soon — or badly.

Denver fans carry on a hot debate over whether Jackson or his teammate, Randy Gradishar, is the more effective linebacker. Nobody really cares what the truth is. There's enough glamour and honor for both of them.

Cornerback
ROGER WEHRLIE
6-0, 190
ST. LOUIS CARDINALS

What you want in an All-Pro cornerback is a guy who plays tough defense against both the run and pass. A vicious tackler when he zeroes in on the ball carrier. A swift, savvy pick-off artist when the ball is in the air anywhere in his zone. What you have with those talents is Roger Wehrlie.

Year after year Roger gets RESPECT from the opposition. They know he has mastered every phase of cornerback play and puts it all on the line every week. He never has a poor game.

Wherlie is one more of those rarities in the NFL who starred as a rookie. A first-round draft choice back in 1969, the Missouri graduate impressed his pro coaches right away. At Missouri he had been an All-America defensive back as a senior; the year before he led the nation in punt-return yardage.

In 1970, a year after his rookie season with the Cardinals, Wehrlie made All-Pro, and has since been up there with the best, except for 1972 when he was out with a knee injury.

"He doesn't look spectacular," says one veteran NFL observer, "but you just can't count on Wehrlie to make a mistake, mentally or physically. When he gets beat on a play it's only because the offensive guy has made an absolutely super, super play."

Just to keep the record straight, he pronounces his name WERE-lee.

Cornerback
ROLLAND LAWRENCE
5-10, 179
ATLANTA FALCONS

How obscure can things be? Rolland Lawrence played at Tabor College. Not meaning to insult Tabor, but we had to

look it up. It's in Kansas. Its football field
seats fewer than 1,500 people. Not many of
them were scouts who came to see Lawrence play.

But Rolland Lawrence talked the Falcons into signing him as a free agent. All
he wanted was a chance. After all, he'd
been that rare thing — a two-way starter.
And he'd racked up 4,000 yards on offense.
The Falcons looked at some of his college
game films and figured they had nothing
to lose. No money was involved unless
Lawrence made the team.

Wow, did he ever make the team! The
Falcons kept him on and he got into all 14
games in his rookie year as a cornerback.
The following season he was a solid starter. By 1975 he had set a new Falcon team
record with nine pass interceptions. In
1976 he was busy enough to set an NFL
mark of 54 punt returns.

This past season, although he's one of
the little guys among NFL cornerbacks, he
was hailed as a terrific hitter. His back-
pedaling against the pass was nimble
and sure. Nobody was getting behind him.
And suddenly the coaches throughout the
league were seeing him as an NFL star,
not just a Falcon leader.

Lawrence says he had to wear a
nametag at home when he was a boy. All
his brothers and sisters did because there
were 10 boys and four girls. He doesn't
need a nametag, now. Everyone knows
who that number 22 is.

Free Safety
CLIFF HARRIS
6-1, 190
DALLAS COWBOYS

Cliff Harris is not only a free safety, but he looks like a free spirit out there. The free safety has a little more latitude in his coverage than the strong safety. Sometimes he even seems to go just where his instincts tell him the running play or the pass is coming. So there's Cliff Harris all over the place.

You'd have to say Harris made All-Pro the hard way. In the first place, he played for Ouachita (pronounced WASH-e-taw) Baptist College in Arkadelphia, Ark. Not many pro scouts know the airline schedules to Arkadelphia. So Harris had no pro teams searching him out. But he asked the Cowboys for a chance in 1970 and signed on as a free agent.

Harris, a tremendous hitter, became an instant starter. But then he was called into military service and had to begin all over again when he came back. Same story. Regained his starting job immediately.

Harris is a master at psyching the receivers he has to cover. "I love to play a mental game with them," he says. "If you step in front of a receiver and make an interception he'll just be a little upset. But if you blast him and really spin his helmet around and ring his bell, he'll be looking for you from then on. He'll lose some of his concentration for the ball.

"Sometimes," he continues, "I even talk to them. I ask them, 'Is it worth it?' It sinks in and makes my job a bit easier."

And nobody makes it look easier than Harris.

Safety
CHARLIE WATERS
6-2, 198
DALLAS COWBOYS

Most fans figured Cliff Harris would be a repeater as an All-Pro, but a lot of them have been wondering why the experts

46

haven't gotten around to Cliff's buddy in the Cowboy secondary. Finally, the experts did get around to strong safety Charlie Waters. The strong safety doesn't have the freedom to roam as much as the free safety; he also must concern himself with the enemy's tight end. And because tight ends are so big, the strong safety has to be extra tough.

Charlie was simply sensational in the job he did last year. "I've never seen an athlete concentrate the way he did," said Dallas coach Tom Landry. "I guess he decided, after eight years in the league, that he wanted that All-Pro label very much. I can't recall a safety hitting as hard as he did, and I can't remember the last mistake he made in his coverage." Other coaches and the sports writers felt that way, too.

Waters never dreamed nine years ago that he'd ever play safety in the NFL. He'd divided his time at Clemson University as a quarterback and wide receiver. His QB experience came in handy when Dallas made him a third-round draft choice and moved him into the secondary. He knew what passing and pass routes were all about. Charlie fit in perfectly with his new chores and made the starting lineup as a rookie. "I don't just want to be the best at my job in the eyes of the fans and writers," he says. "I want to be the best in my own eyes."

Don't worry, Charlie. You are.

ALL-ROOKIE OFFENSE 1977

WR: **Billy Waddy,** Los Angeles Rams
WR: **Wesley Walker,** New York Jets
TE: **Don Hasselbeck,** New England Patriots
 T: **Warren Bryant,** Atlanta Falcons
 T: **Ted Albrecht,** Chicago Bears
 G: **George Reihner,** Houston Oilers
 G: **R.C. Thielemann,** Atlanta Falcons
 C: **Bob Rush,** San Diego Chargers
 Q: **Tommy Kramer,** Minnesota Vikings
RB: **Tony Dorsett,** Dallas Cowboys
RB: **Rob Carpenter,** Houston Oilers

Wide Receiver
BILLY WADDY
5-11, 185
LOS ANGELES RAMS

When the Rams drafted Billy Waddy in the second round, they knew they'd be getting the fastest man the club ever had.... Waddy, a wingback and split end at University of Colorado, runs the 40-yard dash in 4.4, just one step away from flying.... The Rams knew he wasn't big, but with that speed, good hands, and tricky moves, he could pull in a lot of Pat Haden's passes.... Which Billy did. NFL cornerbacks and safetys immediately knew they had something to worry about.... His first year stats of 23 catches for 355 yards are evidence to that. Just wait till Waddy grows up in the pro game and learns his enemy's defensive weaknesses!

Wide Receiver
WESLEY WALKER
6-0, 172
NEW YORK JETS

The Jets knew they were getting a super athlete in Wesley Walker.... At the University of California he was the first four-year two-sport man in more than 40 years. ...A football and track star, he set an  NCAA record for career average pass reception of 25.7 yards per catch. With his great speed and nifty hands, Jet scouts had high hopes for him.... Walker didn't disturb their dream.... Richard Todd, the Jets' QB, soon found that Walker also knew how to run pass routes and get free of the stickiest defenders.... And even though he only weighs 172 pounds, he was tough enough to take the hardest hits the defenders dished out.... When Todd, also a youngster, develops more, Walker will be even better.

50

Tight End
DON HASSELBECK
6-7, 245
NEW ENGLAND PATRIOTS

What a target! At 6 feet 7 inches and 245 pounds, Don Hasselbeck is a quarterback's dream at tight end.... If he gets loose, how can you miss him? The University of Colorado All-America was a starter as a freshman for the Buffalos, and the Patriots lost little time in making him a number 2 draft pick and getting him into the lineup.... Hasselbeck immediately proved he was a great blocker, too, even against those big savvy NFL tackles.... On short-yardage running plays the Patriot coaches were always confident that Hasselbeck would come through.... And few newcomers were as slick at putting a block on the defender and then slipping off to run a pass route.

Tackle
WARREN BRYANT
6-6, 275
ATLANTA FALCONS

Ever since Warren Bryant was a high school freshman folks said: "They'll never push him around." And nobody did.... As a collegian he made Kentucky's starting lineup as a freshman.... With  his size and brute strength he made All-America as a senior and led the Wildcats to their first bowl game in 25 years.... Taken by the Falcons in the first round of the draft, Bryant went to camp and soon proved his they-can't-push-me-around status.... By mid-season everyone around the NFL was predicting big things for him.... He was blocking and pass-protecting like a veteran, rarely missing an assignment.... Of course, people who are 6-6 and 275 pounds often have their own way.

TED ALBRECHT
6-4, 260
CHICAGO BEARS

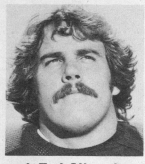

The first pick the Bears made in the 1977 draft was a 260-pound guy who could run the 40 in 4.8. That's super speed for a lineman.... The Bears knew what they were doing when they took Ted Albrecht, another Bear from University of California where he had started 33 straight games.... An All-America tackle, Albrecht was switched to guard in three or four post-season all-star games, but the Chicago Bears put him back at tackle in pro camp.... They liked all that blocking bulk that moved so swiftly off the ball.... And they liked his "quick feet" when he dropped back on pass protection.... What they liked were the things that go into an eventual All-Pro.

Guard
GEORGE REIHNER
6-4, 263
HOUSTON OILERS

The toughest positions to learn in pro football are the offensive guard and tackle spots....Because of the complex pro offenses, the blocking assignments must be learned perfectly.  ...And a rookie doesn't usually get the hang of things for a couple of years....Not so for George Reihner, the Oilers' second-round draft choice from Penn State....He was not only big and rough, but he was smart....Learned all the tricks of pulling out for wide running plays and the trap plays and pass blocking for his quarterback....Began as a defensive lineman as a Penn State frosh but then started three years at tackle....Oiler coaches saw his quickness and versatile blocking ability and said, "This guy is a natural-born pro guard!" Opposing defenders agree.

R.C. THIELEMANN
6-4, 247
ATLANTA FALCONS

R.C. Thielemann, like his Falcon all-rookie teammate Warren Bryant, was a freshman starter in college. . . . At Arkansas, by the time he graduated, he was one of the nation's best interior linemen, and Atlanta tabbed him in the second round of the draft. They figured he could play either guard or center. . . . It turned out to be guard and, with his quickness, Thielemann quickly mastered the job of pulling out to lead sweeps or trapping enemy tackles. . . . His big complaint in pro football is that so many people misspell his name. "They're always leaving out the second 'e' or the last 'n.'" Just so long as they don't leave you out of the all-star lineups, right, R.C.?

Center
BOB RUSH
6-5, 255
SAN DIEGO CHARGERS

Centers rarely make the pro "varsity" in their rookie year....But Charger coach, Tommy Prothro, said: "Rush is the best center I've seen in the draft in all my years in pro ball...." And so the  Chargers simply made him the first offensive lineman they'd drafted in the first round in 15 years....Pro teams rarely do that unless they're convinced they're getting something super....Rush, from Memphis State, was faced with one of the toughest jobs in pro ball—making the snap to the QB and then instantly coming off the ball to make a block on the massive defensive tackle playing right on his nose....Bob Rush did it so well that enemy teams could hardly believe he was a rookie.

Quarterback
TOMMY KRAMER
6-1, 199
MINNESOTA VIKINGS

Rookie quarterbacks don't beat out people like Fran Tarkenton. . . . Nor did Tommy Kramer do that at Minnesota. But when the Vikings' great QB went down with an injury, Kramer got his chance. . . . He was ready for it, as his background predicted. . . . A unanimous All-America at Rice, in Texas, Kramer led the NCAA in total offense and passing in his senior year. . . . His 3,317 yards in the air was the second highest total in NCAA history. . . . Completed 507 of 1,036 passes for 6,197 yards and 37 TDs for his college career. . . . Kramer, smart and with a rifle arm, shared duties last year with Bob Lee after Tarkenton was hurt. . . . And he should take over when Tark finally retires. In his rookie season he hit a nice 52.6 percentage on 30 for 57.

Running Back
TONY DORSETT
5-11, 192
DALLAS COWBOYS

Woosh! There he goes! That was Tony Dorsett who put a move on the enemy linebacker and left him clutching at empty air.... The Cowboys' young super-runner will be doing that for many years to come.... Tom Landry, the Dallas coach, figured Tony would deliver as promised.... This speedster with perfect balance had set an all-time NCAA record of 6,082 yards rushing in his four-year career at Pitt.... Plus 58 TDs.... He was also the first player to have three 1,500 yard-plus seasons.... As a first-year pro he gained 1,007 yards and tallied 13 TDs for the Cowboys. Next stop: All-Pro.

Some fans were surprised when Rob Carpenter beat out the Broncos' Rob Lyttle for the other running back spot opposite Tony Dorsett.... But the pro coaches weren't surprised. A third-round draft pick, Carpenter had been a star at Miami of Ohio, where he rushed for more than 1,000 yards in each of his last two seasons...."But is he fast enough for the NFL?" was the big question.... Carpenter didn't show blazing speed, but his slashing, hard-nosed running style got him more yards than a lot of faster backs in the NFL.... Bum Phillips, the Oiler coach, says: "You rarely see such intensity in a runner. He gets hit but he also gets that extra yard." In his first pro season he racked up 652 of them.

ALL-ROOKIE DEFENSE 1977

E: **Mike Butler**, Green Bay Packers
E: **A.J. Duhe**, Miami Dolphins
T: **Eddie Edwards**, Cincinnati Bengals
T: **Bob Baumhower**, Miami Dolphins
LB: **Kim Bokamper**, Miami Dolphins
LB: **Bob Brudzinski**, Los Angeles Rams
LB: **Terry Beeson**, Seattle Seahawks
CB: **Gary Green**, Kansas City Chiefs
CB: **Ray Clayborn**, New England Patriots
S: **Bill Currier**, Houston Oilers
S: **Vern Roberson**, Miami Dolphins

Defensive End
MIKE BUTLER
6-5, 265
GREEN BAY PACKERS

By the time Mike Butler was a junior at the University of Kansas, opposing coaches stopped trying to run at Mike Butler's end position. After all, when you are 6-5, 265 pounds, and quick as a cat, and like to devour ball carriers—well, you get the picture....As a first-round draft choice, Butler carried the same talents into the Packers' training camp....It wasn't long into the regular season when opposing offenses knew they were going to have trouble with this rookie.... "It's amazing how quick he made the pro adjustment," said Packer coach, Bart Starr....The betting is that Mike Butler will be an All-Pro no later than his third season.

Defensive End
A. J. DUHE
6-4, 247
MIAMI DOLPHINS

The Dolphins knew what they were doing when they made A.J. Duhe their number-one draft pick....He'd been a four-year starting tackle at Louisiana State, from his first day as a freshman, and averaged 72 tackles per season....He was also a top student, being able to speak in the Cajun dialect of French-background Louisiana....But the Dolphins, noting his speed and agility, shifted him to defensive end and he became an instant starter with the pros, just as he had been in college....The enemy found him a tough man to block out of a play and QBs found him an absolute problem when he put on a pass rush....Next stop: All-Pro?

Defensive Tackle
EDDIE EDWARDS
6-5, 250
CINCINNATI BENGALS

The Bengals' front office had no doubts about their first draft choice last year. "Eddie Edwards is the fastest and strongest defensive lineman in sight," said their director of player personnel. ...He was talking about Miami of Florida's All-America tackle who had more than 100 tackles in his senior year....Edwards was the sprinter type with great arm strength....Which meant he could shuck off blockers and get to the passer—pronto! The pros found him just as tough to hold out of the action, whether they were trying to run over his position or keep him off the QB on pass plays....Instant pro stardom was the name of the game for Edwards.

Defensive Tackle
BOB BAUMHOWER
6-5, 258
MIAMI DOLPHINS

The Dolphins' defensive Front Four is shaping up very well for the future.... With All-Rookie A.J. Duhe at one end, and Bob Baumhower at a tackle, things are looking up.... Baumhower, a three-year  starter at Alabama, was a second-round draft choice with Miami.... "We needed to improve our pass rush against opposing quarterbacks," said coach Don Shula.... In Baumhower, the Dolphins not only got a towering pass rusher but a fierce defender against the run.... At Alabama he was noted for the number of times he tossed enemy carriers for losses and in his first pro season he seemed to make it a continuing habit.

KIM BOKAMPER
6-6, 245
MIAMI DOLPHINS

The Dolphins were very high on Kim Bokamper when they made him a first-round draft choice, from San Jose State, in 1976....But their hopes for him were put off for a year when he tore up a knee in a pre-season game in 1976. ...Then came the question in the 1977 pre-season camp: Would he be fully recovered from his operation—retain his 4.7 speed?...NFL ball carriers throughout the league got the answer, too.... Bokamper showed no drop-off in speed or agility as he roamed his linebacking area, plugging any holes the front four left, viciously dumping the runners and batting down passes....And at 6 feet 6 inches it's like passing over a tree.

Linebacker
BOB BRUDZINSKI
6-4, 230
LOS ANGELES RAMS

Bob Brudzinski, an All-America defensive end from Ohio State, had a career total of 214 tackles and assists—one of the highest in Buckeye history....In making him a first-round draft choice, the Rams figured anyone that active should become an outside linebacker. They were right.... Brudzinski was a natural and staked out a regular job for himself.... The tall rookie linebacker soon became one of the slickest at dropping back on pass defense, where his size and long reach made it hazardous for opposing QBs to flip the ball anywhere near him. ...Smart and fast, the former Buckeye is a good bet for All-Pro in the not too distant future.

Linebacker
TERRY BEESON
6-3, 240
SEATTLE SEAHAWKS

By now the Dallas Cowboys are sorry they traded Terry Beeson to the Seahawks as a second-round draft choice. ...At least they should have taken a good look at the big Kansas linebacker who led the Jayhawks in tackles in his last two years.... A four-year starter, ever since his freshman year, Beeson also had plenty of "smarts," which was natural for a guy majoring in chemical engineering.... With the Seahawks, Beeson immediately added some savage tackling to his brains and almost immediately won a starting role.... Coaches throughout the NFL predict a sensational future for Beeson...."He doesn't fool easily and his agility gets him out of any mistake he makes," said one coach.

Cornerback
GARY GREEN
5-11, 184
KANSAS CITY CHIEFS

The Chiefs' scouts were sure that Gary Green was the third-best college player in the draft, behind Tony Dorsett and Ricky Bell.... So they drafted him on the first round, hoping nobody else would get to him before they did.... They were lucky.... Pro teams picking before them weren't bothering with defensive backs as early choices.... So the Chiefs got the All-America who made a specialty of intercepting enemy passes and coming up fast to dump ball carriers.... Rookie defensive backs are supposed to take time to learn their trade in the NFL, but throughout the league, coaches were saying things like: "How'd this guy get here so soon?"

RAY CLAYBORN
6-1, 181
NEW ENGLAND PATRIOTS

At the University of Texas, Ray Clayborn started out as a running back. And why not, with blazing 9.4 speed in the 100-yard dash? He starred as a halfback in his freshman and sophomore seasons, but his coaches told him they needed help in the defensive secondary.... So, Clayborn, a real team player, consented to move to defense. What a move! Among other things, as a senior he had TD punt returns of 64, 65, and 85 yards.... When the Patriots drafted him in the opening round, they also were convinced he had a great ability to read offensive patterns.... They were right. Clayborn, with his sizzling speed, had great defensive range. ...Another fine Patriot defender to go with their brilliant Mike Haynes and Tim Fox, who were All-Rookie two years ago.

Safety
BILL CURRIER
6-0, 190
HOUSTON OILERS

Oiler officials were frankly surprised when they found the prize package they had plucked out of the ninth round in the draft.... Ninth-round draft choices are supposed to be after-

thoughts. They rarely make the pro "varsity." ... But Currier had been a three-year defensive starter at South Carolina and played in the Blue-Gray all-star game line.... And he turned out to be one of those "just-give-me-a-chance-and-get-out-of-my-way" kinds of guys... .In pro camp he hounded receivers like a ghost and knocked ball carriers silly. ...It wasn't long before Houston coaches knew they had to keep him around.... His first-year play as a pro proved they were right.

70

VERN ROBERSON
6-2, 195
MIAMI DOLPHINS

When a player comes to a pro team as a free agent, it means no club thought him good enough to waste a draft pick on. . . . All the free agent wants is for somebody to take a look at him, at no cost. . . . Vern Roberson, from Grambling College, said, "Take a look.". . . The Dolphins did. . . . The big, swift safety hit ball carriers like a ton of bricks and batted down passes like a veteran. . . . "What a nose for the ball," said the Dolphin coaches, and got him into the starting lineup as soon as they could. . . . Around the league the enemy was saying: "Where'd HE come from!" Usually as Vern was separating them from their senses.

1977 FINAL STANDINGS
AMERICAN FOOTBALL
CONFERENCE

EASTERN DIVISION

	W	L	T	Pct.	Pts.	OP
*Baltimore	10	4	0	.714	295	221
Miami	10	4	0	.714	313	197
New England	9	5	0	.643	278	217
New York	3	11	0	.214	191	300
Buffalo	3	11	0	.214	160	313

WESTERN DIVISION

	W	L	T	Pct.	Pts.	OP
*Denver	12	2	0	.857	274	148
#Oakland	11	3	0	.786	351	230
San Diego	7	7	0	.500	222	205
Seattle	5	9	0	.357	282	373
Kansas City	2	12	0	.143	225	349

CENTRAL DIVISION

	W	L	T	Pct.	Pts.	OP
*Pittsburgh	9	5	0	.643	283	243
Houston	8	6	0	.571	299	230
Cincinnati	8	6	0	.571	238	235
Cleveland	6	8	0	.429	269	267

*Division Winner
#Wild Card for Playoffs

AFC Playoffs
Oakland 37, Baltimore 31 (Double O'T)
Dallas 34, Pittsburgh 21

AFC Championship
Denver 20, Oakland 17

Super Bowl XII
Dallas 27, Denver 10

and Previews for 1978...

Baltimore Colts

John Dutton...The big defensive end is a tower of strength up front.

QUARTERBACKING:
RUNNING:
RECEIVING:
OFFENSIVE LINE:
DEFENSE:

Miami Dolphins

Ben Malone...Hard-nosed runner who provides balance for Griese's passes.

QUARTERBACKING:
RUNNING:
RECEIVING:
OFFENSIVE LINE:
DEFENSE:

73

New England Patriots

Steve Grogan...QB has to regain his '76 form for Pats to be a threat.

QUARTERBACKING:
RUNNING:
RECEIVING:
OFFENSIVE LINE:
DEFENSE:

Buffalo Bills

Joe Ferguson...With O.J. gone, the Bills' QB has to be a real hero.

QUARTERBACKING:
RUNNING:
RECEIVING:
OFFENSIVE LINE:
DEFENSE:

74

New York Jets

Richard Todd...Still a young QB but he may turn the Jets around.

QUARTERBACKING: 🏈 🏈
RUNNING: 🏈 🏈
RECEIVING: 🏈 🏈 🏈
OFFENSIVE LINE: 🏈 🏈 🏈
DEFENSE: 🏈 🏈

WESTERN DIVISION

Oakland Raiders

Fred Biletnikoff...The Raider wide receiver still has the niftiest moves.

QUARTERBACKING: 🏈 🏈 🏈 🏈 ◗
RUNNING: 🏈 🏈 🏈 🏈 ◗
RECEIVING: 🏈 🏈 🏈 🏈 🏈
OFFENSIVE LINE: 🏈 🏈 🏈 🏈 🏈
DEFENSE: 🏈 🏈 🏈 🏈

Denver Broncos

Riley Odoms...Tight end who is hard to bring down after catching ball.

QUARTERBACKING:
RUNNING:
RECEIVING:
OFFENSIVE LINE:
DEFENSE:

San Diego Chargers

Louie Kelcher...May soon be recognized as an All-Pro defensive tackle.

QUARTERBACKING:
RUNNING:
RECEIVING:
OFFENSIVE LINE:
DEFENSE:

76

Kansas City Chiefs

Charlie Getty... Young guard is rapidly developing into super blocker.

QUARTERBACKING:
RUNNING:
RECEIVING:
OFFENSIVE LINE:
DEFENSE:

Seattle Seahawks

Steve Largent... The Seahawk receiver flies among the league's best.

QUARTERBACKING:
RUNNING:
RECEIVING:
OFFENSIVE LINE:
DEFENSE:

CENTRAL DIVISION

Pittsburgh Steelers

Jack Lambert...The great linebacker puts muscle in Steeler defense.

QUARTERBACKING:	🏈 🏈 🏈 🏈
RUNNING:	🏈 🏈 🏈 🏈
RECEIVING:	🏈 🏈 🏈 🏈 ◖
OFFENSIVE LINE:	🏈 🏈 🏈 🏈
DEFENSE:	🏈 🏈 🏈 🏈

Houston Oilers

Ken Burrough...This wide receiver is one of the niftiest in the NFL.

QUARTERBACKING:	🏈 🏈 🏈 ◖
RUNNING:	🏈 🏈 🏈 ◖
RECEIVING:	🏈 🏈 🏈 🏈
OFFENSIVE LINE:	🏈 🏈
DEFENSE:	🏈 🏈 🏈 🏈 ◖

Cincinnati Bengals

Ken Anderson...If the QB regains his touch, the Bengals will really roar.

QUARTERBACKING:	
RUNNING:	
RECEIVING:	
OFFENSIVE LINE:	
DEFENSE:	

Cleveland Browns

Jerry Sherk...There are few better defensive tackles than this one.

QUARTERBACKING:	
RUNNING:	
RECEIVING:	
OFFENSIVE LINE:	
DEFENSE:	

1977 FINAL STANDINGS NATIONAL FOOTBALL CONFERENCE

EASTERN DIVISION

	W	L	T	Pct.	Pts.	OP
*Dallas	12	2	0	.857	345	212
Washington	9	5	0	.643	196	189
St. Louis	7	7	0	.500	272	287
Philadelphia	5	9	0	.357	220	207
New York Giants	5	9	0	.357	181	265

WESTERN DIVISION

	W	L	T	Pct.	Pts.	OP
*Los Angeles	10	4	0	.714	302	146
Atlanta	7	7	0	.500	179	129
San Francisco	5	9	0	.357	220	260
New Orleans	3	11	0	.214	232	336

CENTRAL DIVISION

	W	L	T	Pct.	Pts.	OP
*Minnesota	9	5	0	.643	231	227
#Chicago	9	5	0	.643	255	253
Detroit	6	8	0	.429	183	252
Green Bay	4	10	0	.286	134	219
Tampa Bay	2	12	0	.143	103	223

*Division Champion
#Wild Card for Playoffs

NFC Playoffs
Dallas 37, Chicago 7
Minnesota 14, Los Angeles 7

NFC Championship
Dallas 23, Minnesota 6

Super Bowl XII
Dallas 27, Denver 10

and Previews for 1978...

Dallas Cowboys

Randy White... His quickness marks his exceptional skill as defensive tackle.

QUARTERBACKING:
RUNNING:
RECEIVING:
OFFENSIVE LINE:
DEFENSE:

Washington Redskins

Bill Kilmer... An aging QB whose skills still keep Redskins in the fight.

QUARTERBACKING:
RUNNING:
RECEIVING:
OFFENSIVE LINE:
DEFENSE:

New York Giants

Jack Gregory... The veteran end is steadying influence on Giant defense.

QUARTERBACKING:
RUNNING:
RECEIVING:
OFFENSIVE LINE:
DEFENSE:

St. Louis Cardinals

Jim Hart... The QB may lead the Cards back from last year's fall-off.

QUARTERBACKING:
RUNNING:
RECEIVING:
OFFENSIVE LINE:
DEFENSE:

Philadelphia Eagles

Ron Jaworski...Eagles may fly higher this year on his strong arm.

QUARTERBACKING:	🏈 🏈
RUNNING:	🏈 🏈 ◖
RECEIVING:	🏈 🏈
OFFENSIVE LINE:	🏈 🏈
DEFENSE:	🏈 🏈 🏈

WESTERN DIVISION

Los Angeles Rams

Pat Haden...With Namath gone, he really has the QB job all to himself.

QUARTERBACKING:	🏈 🏈 🏈
RUNNING:	🏈 🏈 🏈 🏈 ◖
RECEIVING:	🏈 🏈 🏈
OFFENSIVE LINE:	🏈 🏈 🏈
DEFENSE:	🏈 🏈 🏈 🏈 ◖

San Francisco 49ers

Delvin Williams...The 49ers' best bet for the tough yardage on the ground.

QUARTERBACKING:
RUNNING:
RECEIVING:
OFFENSIVE LINE:
DEFENSE:

Atlanta Falcons

Greg Brezina...Veteran linebacker is one of few defensive stalwarts.

QUARTERBACKING:
RUNNING:
RECEIVING:
OFFENSIVE LINE:
DEFENSE:

New Orleans Saints

Chuck Muncie...Wherever Saints go on ground, he'll have to take them there.

QUARTERBACKING:	🏈 🏈
RUNNING:	🏈 🏈 🏈
RECEIVING:	🏈 🏈 🏈
OFFENSIVE LINE:	🏈 🏈 ◖
DEFENSE:	🏈 🏈 ◖

CENTRAL DIVISION

Minnesota Vikings

Chuck Foreman...Has to carry Vikings' ground game almost by himself.

QUARTERBACKING:	🏈 🏈 🏈 🏈
RUNNING:	🏈 🏈 🏈
RECEIVING:	🏈 🏈 🏈
OFFENSIVE LINE:	🏈 🏈 🏈 ◖
DEFENSE:	🏈 🏈 🏈 🏈

Chicago Bears

Revie Sorey...One of the better pulling guards and blockers in the NFL.

QUARTERBACKING:	
RUNNING:	
RECEIVING:	
OFFENSIVE LINE:	
DEFENSE:	

Detroit Lions

Dick Jauron...Former Ivy star is one of the league's tougher defensive backs.

QUARTERBACKING:

RUNNING:

RECEIVING:

OFFENSIVE LINE:

DEFENSE:

Green Bay Packers

Johnnie Gray . . . He has to hold together the Packers' secondary.

QUARTERBACKING:	
RUNNING:	
RECEIVING:	
OFFENSIVE LINE:	
DEFENSE:	

Tampa Bay Buccaneers

Ricky Bell . . . If only the Bucs had a line to open some holes for him!

QUARTERBACKING:
RUNNING:
RECEIVING:
OFFENSIVE LINE:
DEFENSE:

HOW THEY'RE PICKED
TO FINISH IN 1978

AFC

East	West	Central
1. Baltimore	1. Oakland	1. Pittsburgh
2. Miami	2. Denver	2. Houston
3. New England	3. San Diego	3. Cincinnati
4. Buffalo	4. Kansas City	4. Cleveland
5. New York Jets	5. Seattle	

NFC

East	West	Central
1. Dallas	1. Los Angeles	1. Minnesota
2. Washington	2. San Francisco	2. Chicago
3. New York Giants	3. Atlanta	3. Detroit
4. St. Louis	4. New Orleans	4. Green Bay ✓
5. Philadelphia		5. Tampa Bay

Super Bowl XIII
Oakland vs. Los Angeles or Dallas

Best Bet for
Rookie-of-the-Year
Earl Campbell, Houston

1977 RECORDS

SCORING

INDIVIDUAL CHAMPION
AFC: 99 Errol Mann, Oakland (kicker)
NFC: 96 Walter Payton, Chicago

TOUCHDOWNS
AFC: 13 Nat Moore, Miami (1 Rushing; 12 Receptions)
NFC: 16 Walter Payton, Chicago (14 Rushing; 2 Receptions)

EXTRA POINTS
AFC: 39 Errol Mann, Oakland (42 Attempts)
NFC: 39 Efren Herrera, Dallas (41 Attempts)

FIELD GOALS
AFC: 20 Errol Mann, Oakland (28 Attempts)
NFC: 21 Mark Moseley, Washington (37 Attempts)

ONE GAME PERFORMANCE
AFC: 18 (3 TDs) Nat Moore, Miami (2) vs San Francisco, September 25 & vs St. Louis, November 24; Larry Poole, Cleveland vs Pittsburgh, November 13
NFC: 24 (4 TDs) Wayne Morris, St. Louis vs New Orleans, October 23

TEAM LEADERS
AFC: BALTIMORE 83 Toni Linhart; BUFFALO 34 Carson Long; CINCINNATI 82 Chris Bahr; CLEVELAND 81 Don Cockroft; DENVER 76 Jim Turner; HOUSTON 55 Toni Fritsch; KANSAS CITY 51 Jan Stenerud; MIAMI 78 Nat Moore; NEW ENGLAND 78 John Smith; NEW YORK JETS 63 Pat Leahy; OAKLAND 99 Errol Mann; PITTSBURGH 66 Franco Harris; SAN DIEGO 72 Rolf Benirschke; SEATTLE 60 Steve Largent & John Leypoldt

NFC: ATLANTA 36 Haskel Stanback; CHICAGO 96 Walter Payton;
DALLAS 93 Efren Herrera; DETROIT 43 Steve Mike-Mayer;
GREEN BAY 50 Chester Marcol; LOS ANGELES 86 Rafael Septien;
MINNESOTA 54 Chuck Foreman & Sammy White; NEW ORLEANS
54 Henry Childs; NEW YORK GIANTS 61 Joe Danelo;
PHILADELPHIA 42 Harold Carmichael; ST. LOUIS 56 Jim Bakken;
SAN FRANCISCO 54 Delvin Williams; TAMPA BAY 20 Allan
Leavitt; WASHINGTON 82 Mark Moseley

TEAM CHAMPION

AFC: 351   Oakland
NFC: 345   Dallas

TOP TEN SCORERS—TOUCHDOWNS

	TDs Tot	TDs Rush	TDs Pass	TDs Misc	Tot Pts
Payton, Walter, Chi.	16	14	2	0	96
Dorsett, Tony, Dall.	13	12	1	0	78
Moore, Nat, Mia.	13	1	12	0	78
Harris, Franco, Pitt.	11	11	0	0	66
Largent, Steve, Sea.	10	0	10	0	60
Childs, Henry, N.O.	9	0	9	0	54
Foreman, Chuck, Minn.	9	6	3	0	54
McCutcheon, Lawrence, L.A.	9	7	2	0	54
Morris, Wayne, St.L.	9	8	1	0	54
White, Sammy. Minn.	9	0	9	0	54

TOP TEN SCORERS—KICKING

	XP Made	XP Att	FG Made	FG Att	Tot Pts
Mann, Errol, Oak.	39	42	20	28	99
Herrera, Efren, Dall.	39	41	18	29	93
Septien, Rafael, L.A..	32	35	18	30	86
Linhart, Toni, Balt.	32	35	17	26	83
Bahr, Chris, Cin.	25	26	19	27	82
Moseley, Mark, Wash.	19	19	21	37	82
Cockroft, Don, Clev.	30	31	17	23	81

	XP Made	XP Att	FG Made	FG Att	Tot Pts
Smith, John, N.E.	33	33	15	21	78
Benirschke, Rolf, S.D.	21	24	17	23	72
Turner, Jim, Den.	31	34	13	19	*70

*Not including one TD scored on reception

AFC—INDIVIDUALS

	TDs	TDR	TDP	TDM	XP	XPA	FG	FGA	PTS
Mann, Errol, Oak. ...	0	0	0	0	39	42	20	28	99
Linhart, Toni, Balt. ..	0	0	0	0	32	35	17	26	83
Bahr, Chris, Cin.	0	0	0	0	25	26	19	27	82
Cockroft, Don, Clev. .	0	0	0	0	30	31	17	23	81
Moore, Nat, Mia.	13	1	12	0	0	0	0	0	78
Smith, John, N.E. ...	0	0	0	0	33	33	15	21	78
Turner, Jim, Den. ...	1	0	1	0	31	34	13	19	76
Benirschke, Rolf, S.D.	0	0	0	0	21	24	17	23	72
Yepremian, Garo, Mia.	0	0	0	0	37	40	10	22	67
Harris, Franco, Pitt. ..	11	11	0	0	0	0	0	0	66
Leahy, Pat, N.Y.J.	0	0	0	0	18	21	15	25	63

NFC—INDIVIDUALS

	TDs	TDR	TDP	TDM	XP	XPA	FG	FGA	PTS
Payton, Walter, Chi. .	16	14	2	0	0	0	0	0	96
Herrera, Efren, Dall. .	0	0	0	0	39	41	18	29	93
Septien, Rafael, L.A. .	0	0	0	0	32	35	18	30	86
Moseley, Mark, Wash.	0	0	0	0	19	19	21	37	82
Dorsett, Tony, Dall. ..	13	12	1	0	0	0	0	0	78
Thomas, Bob, Chi. ..	0	0	0	0	27	30	14	27	69
Danelo, Joe, N.Y.G. .	0	0	0	0	19	20	14	23	61
Bakken, Jim, St.L. ..	0	0	0	0	35	36	7	16	56
Childs, Henry, N.O. ..	9	0	9	0	0	0	0	0	54
Foreman, Chuck, Minn.	9	6	3	0	0	0	0	0	54
McCutcheon, Lawrence, L.A. ...	9	7	2	0	0	0	0	0	54

RUSHING

INDIVIDUAL CHAMPION
AFC: 1,273 (Yards)   Mark van Eeghen, Oakland
NFC: 1,852 (Yards)   Walter Payton, Chicago

AVERAGE
AFC: 4.8 (Yards)   Benny Malone, Miami (615 Yards; 129 Attempts)
NFC: 5.5 (Yards)   Walter Payton, Chicago (1,852 Yards; 339 Attempts)

TOUCHDOWNS
AFC: 11   Franco Harris, Pittsburgh
NFC: 14   Walter Payton, Chicago

ATTEMPTS
AFC: 324   Mark van Eeghen, Oakland
NFC: 339   Walter Payton, Chicago

LONGEST
AFC: 78 (Yards)   Greg Pruitt, Cleveland vs Kansas City, October 30 (TD)
NFC: 84 (Yards)   Tony Dorsett, Dallas vs Philadelphia, December 4 (TD)

ONE GAME PERFORMANCE
AFC: 179 (Yards; 29 Attempts)   Franco Harris, Pittsburgh vs Dallas, November 20
NFC: 275 (Yards; 40 Attempts)   Walter Payton, Chicago vs Minnesota, November 20, NFL record

TEAM LEADERS
AFC: BALTIMORE 1,159 Lydell Mitchell; BUFFALO 557 O.J. Simpson; CINCINNATI 585 Pete Johnson; CLEVELAND 1,086 Greg Pruitt; DENVER 489 Otis Armstrong; HOUSTON 660 Ronnie Coleman; KANSAS CITY 550 Ed Podolak; MIAMI 615 Benny Malone; NEW ENGLAND 1,015 Sam Cunningham; NEW YORK JETS 595 Clark Gaines; OAKLAND 1,273 Mark van

Eeghen; PITTSBURGH 1,162 Franco Harris; SAN DIEGO 543
Rickey Young; SEATTLE 763 Sherman Smith
NFC: ATLANTA 873 Haskel Stanback; CHICAGO 1,852 Walter
Payton; DALLAS 1,007 Tony Dorsett; DETROIT 521 Horace
King; GREEN BAY 554 Barty Smith; LOS ANGELES 1,238
Lawrence McCutcheon; MINNESOTA 1,112 Chuck Foreman;
NEW ORLEANS 811 Chuck Muncie; NEW YORK GIANTS 577
Bob Hammond; PHILADELPHIA 546 Mike Hogan; ST. LOUIS
739 Terry Metcalf; SAN FRANCISCO 931 Delvin Williams;
TAMPA BAY 436 Ricky Bell; WASHINGTON 806 Mike Thomas

TEAM CHAMPION

AFC: 2,627 (Yards)   Oakland (681 Attempts; 3.9 Average)
NFC: 2,811 (Yards)   Chicago (599 Attempts; 4.7 Average)

TOP TEN RUSHERS

	Att	Yards	Avg	Long	TDs
Payton, Walter, Chi.	339	1852	5.5	73	14
van Eeghen, Mark, Oak.	324	1273	3.9	27	7
McCutcheon, Lawrence, L.A. .	294	1238	4.2	48	7
Harris, Franco, Pitt.	300	1162	3.9	t61	11
Mitchell, Lydell, Balt.	301	1159	3.9	t64	3
Foreman, Chuck, Minn.	270	1112	4.1	51	6
Pruitt, Greg, Clev.	236	1086	4.6	t78	3
Cunningham, Sam, N.E.	270	1015	3.8	t31	4
Dorsett, Tony, Dall.	208	1007	4.8	t84	12
Williams, Delvin, S.F.	268	931	3.5	40	7

AFC—INDIVIDUALS

	Att	Yards	Avg	Long	TDs
van Eeghen, Mark, Oak.	324	1273	3.9	27	7
Harris, Franco, Pitt.	300	1162	3.9	t61	11
Mitchell, Lydell, Balt.	301	1159	3.9	t64	3
Pruitt, Greg, Clev.	236	1086	4.6	t78	3
Cunningham, Sam, N.E.	270	1015	3.8	t31	4
Davis, Clarence, Oak.	194	787	4.1	t37	5
Smith, Sherman, Sea.	163	763	4.7	39	4
Miller, Cleo, Clev.	163	756	4.6	38	4

t = Touchdown

	Att	Yards	Avg	Long	TDs
Calhoun, Don, N.E.	198	727	3.7	25	4
Coleman, Ronnie, Hou.	185	660	3.6	22	5
Carpenter, Rob, Hou.	144	652	4.5	77	1
Malone, Benny, Mia.	129	615	4.8	t66	5
Gaines, Clark, N.Y.J.	158	595	3.8	19	3
Johnson, Pete, Cin.	153	585	3.8	65	4

NFC—INDIVIDUALS

	Att	Yards	Avg	Long	TDs
Payton, Walter, Chi.	339	1852	5.5	73	14
McCutcheon, Lawrence, L.A.	294	1238	4.2	48	7
Foreman, Chuck, Minn.	270	1112	4.1	51	6
Dorsett, Tony, Dall.	208	1007	4.8	t84	12
Williams, Delvin, S.F.	268	931	3.5	40	7
Stanback, Haskel, Atl.	247	873	3.5	35	6
Muncie, Chuck, N.O.	201	811	4.0	36	6
Thomas, Mike, Wash.	228	806	3.5	31	3
Jackson, Wilbur, S.F.	179	780	4.4	80	7
Metcalf, Terry, St. L.	149	739	5.0	t62	4
Newhouse, Robert, Dall.	180	721	4.0	29	3
Morris, Wayne, St. L.	165	661	4.0	35	8

AFC—TEAM

	Att	Yards	Avg	Long	TDs
Oakland	681	2,627	3.9	t37	20
Miami	519	2,366	4.6	t77	18
New England	603	2,303	3.8	41	13
Pittsburgh	581	2,258	3.9	t61	20
Cleveland	510	2,200	4.3	t78	9
Baltimore	566	2,123	3.8	t64	17
Denver	523	2,043	3.9	62	16
Houston	509	1,989	3.9	77	15
Seattle	461	1,964	4.3	39	12
Buffalo	450	1,861	4.1	66	3
Cincinnati	488	1,861	3.8	65	10
Kansas City	456	1,843	4.0	59	13

	Att	Yards	Avg	Long	TDs
San Diego	488	1,761	3.6	46	10
New York Jets	437	1,618	3.7	27	6
Conference Total	7,272	28,817	——	t78	182
Conference Average	519.4	2,058.4	4.0	——	13.0

NFC—TEAM

	Att	Yards	Avg	Long	TDs
Chicago	599	2,811	4.7	73	18
Los Angeles	621	2,575	4.1	48	19
Dallas	564	2,369	4.2	t84	21
San Francisco	564	2,086	3.7	80	16
St. Louis	507	2,042	4.0	t62	19
New Orleans	484	2,024	4.2	36	14
New York Giants	548	1,897	3.5	32	11
Atlanta	582	1,890	3.2	35	9
Minnesota	510	1,821	3.6	51	9
Washington	502	1,752	3.5	34	4
Philadelphia	484	1,722	3.6	t70	10
Detroit	479	1,706	3.6	35	11
Green Bay	469	1,464	3.1	40	5
Tampa Bay	465	1,424	3.1	35	4
Conference Total	7,378	27,583	——	t84	170
Conference Average	527.0	1,970.2	3.7	——	12.1

PASSING

INDIVIDUAL CHAMPION
AFC: 88.0 (Rating Points) Bob Griese, Miami
NFC: 87.1 (Rating Points) Roger Staubach, Dallas

ATTEMPTS
AFC: 457 Joe Ferguson, Buffalo
NFC: 361 Roger Staubach, Dallas

COMPLETIONS
AFC: 224 Bert Jones, Baltimore
NFC: 210 Roger Staubach, Dallas

COMPLETION PERCENTAGE
AFC: 58.6 Bob Griese, Miami (307 Attempts; 180 Completions)
NFC: 60.1 Fran Tarkenton, Minnesota (258 Attempts; 155
Completions)

YARDAGE
AFC: 2,803 Joe Ferguson, Buffalo
NFC: 2,620 Roger Staubach, Dallas

TOUCHDOWN PASSES
AFC: 22 Bob Griese, Miami
NFC: 18 Ron Jaworski, Philadelphia
Roger Staubach, Dallas

MOST INTERCEPTIONS
AFC: 24 Joe Ferguson, Buffalo (457 Attempts)
NFC: 21 Ron Jaworski, Philadelphia (346 Attempts)

LOWEST PERCENTAGE, PASSES HAD INTERCEPTED
AFC: 2.8 Bert Jones, Baltimore (393 Attempts; 11 Intercepted)
NFC: 2.5 Roger Staubach, Dallas (361 Attempts; 9 Intercepted)

TEAM CHAMPION
AFC: 86.1 (Rating Points) Miami
NFC: 85.1 (Rating Points) Dallas

TOP TEN INDIVIDUAL QUALIFIERS

	Att	Comp	Pct Comp	Yards	Int	Rating Points
Griese, Bob, Mia.	307	180	58.6	2252	13	88.0
Staubach, Roger, Dall.	361	210	58.2	2620	9	87.1
Haden, Pat, L.A.	216	122	56.5	1551	6	84.4
Morton, Craig, Den.	254	131	51.6	1929	8	82.1
Jones, Bert, Balt.	393	224	57.0	2686	11	80.7
Stabler, Ken, Oak.	294	169	57.5	2176	20	75.2

	Att	Comp	Pct Comp	Yards	Int	Rating Points
Bradshaw, Terry, Pitt.	314	162	51.6	2523	19	71.2
Anderson, Ken, Cin.	323	166	51.4	2145	11	69.8
Tarkenton, Fran, Minn.	258	155	60.1	1734	14	69.3
Landry, Greg, Det.	240	135	56.3	1359	7	68.8

AFC INDIVIDUAL QUALIFIERS

	Att	Comp	Pct Comp	Yards	Int	Rating Points
Griese, Bob, Mia.	307	180	58.6	2252	13	88.0
Morton, Craig, Den.	254	131	51.6	1929	8	82.1
Jones, Bert, Balt.	393	224	57.0	2686	11	80.7
Stabler, Ken, Oak.	294	169	57.5	2176	20	75.2
Bradshaw, Terry, Pitt.	314	162	51.6	2523	19	71.2
Anderson, Ken, Cin.	323	166	51.4	2145	11	69.8
Grogan, Steve, N.E.	305	160	52.5	2162	21	65.3
Pastorini, Dan, Hou.	319	169	53.0	1987	18	62.6
Sipe, Brian, Clev.	195	112	57.4	1233	14	61.6
Todd, Richard, N.Y.J.	265	133	50.2	1863	17	60.6
Livingston, Mike, K.C.	282	143	50.7	1823	15	59.8
Harris, James, S.D.	211	109	51.7	1240	11	56.0

NFC INDIVIDUAL QUALIFIERS

	Att	Comp	Pct Comp	Yards	Int	Rating Points
Staubach, Roger, Dall.	361	210	58.2	2620	9	87.1
Haden, Pat, L.A.	216	122	56.5	1551	6	84.4
Tarkenton, Fran, Minn.	258	155	60.1	1734	14	69.3
Landry, Greg, Det.	240	135	56.3	1359	7	68.8
Manning, Archie, N.O.	205	113	55.1	1284	9	68.8
Kilmer, Bill, Wash.	201	99	49.3	1187	7	66.6
Hart, Jim, St. L.	355	186	52.4	2542	20	64.6
Plunkett, Jim, S.F.	248	128	51.6	1693	14	62.2
Avellini, Bob, Chi.	293	154	52.6	2004	18	61.7
Jaworski, Ron, Phil.	346	166	48.0	2183	21	60.3
Theismann, Joe, Wash.	182	84	46.2	1097	9	58.0

PASS RECEIVING

INDIVIDUAL CHAMPION
AFC: 71   Lydell Mitchell, Baltimore
NFC: 51   Ahmad Rashad, Minnesota

YARDAGE
AFC: 816   Ken Burrough, Houston
NFC: 870   Drew Pearson, Dallas

AVERAGE GAIN
AFC: 21.1   Wesley Walker, New York Jets (35 Receptions; 740 Yards)
NFC: 20.6   Mel Gray, St. Louis (38 Receptions; 782 Yards)

TOUCHDOWNS
AFC: 12   Nat Moore, Miami
NFC: 9   Henry Childs, New Orleans
          Sammy White, Minnesota

LONGEST
AFC: 94 (Yards)   Billy Brooks, Cincinnati vs Minnesota, November 13 (from Ken Anderson, TD)
NFC: 95 (Yards)   Steve Odom, Green Bay vs Minnesota, October 2 (from Lynn Dickey, TD)

ONE GAME PERFORMANCE
AFC: 11   Don McCauley, Baltimore vs Denver, November 27 (112 Yards)
NFC: 9   Tony Galbreath, New Orleans vs San Diego, October 9 (55 Yards)
Morris Owens, Tampa Bay vs Seattle, October 16 (166 Yards)

TEAM LEADERS
AFC: BALTIMORE 71 Lydell Mitchell; BUFFALO 60 Bob Chandler; CINCINNATI 39 Billy Brooks; CLEVELAND 41 Cleo Miller; DENVER 37 Riley Odoms; HOUSTON 43 Ken Burrough; KANSAS CITY 48 Walter White; MIAMI 52 Nat Moore; NEW ENGLAND 42 Sam Cunningham; NEW YORK JETS 55 Clark Gaines; OAKLAND 48

Dave Casper; PITTSBURGH 50 Lynn Swann; SAN DIEGO 48 Rickey Young; SEATTLE 33 Steve Largent

NFC: ATLANTA 39 Alfred Jenkins; CHICAGO 50 James Scott; DALLAS 48 Drew Pearson; DETROIT 40 Horace King; GREEN BAY 37 Barty Smith; LOS ANGELES 48 Harold Jackson; MINNESOTA 51 Ahmad Rashad; NEW ORLEANS 41 Tony Galbreath; NEW YORK GIANTS 22 Jimmy Robinson; PHILADELPHIA 46 Harold Carmichael; ST. LOUIS 40 Ike Harris; SAN FRANCISCO 32 Gene Washington; TAMPA BAY 34 Morris Owens; WASHINGTON 36 Jean Fugett

TOP TEN PASS RECEIVERS

	No	Yards	Avg	Long	TDs
Mitchell, Lydell, Balt.	71	620	8.7	38	4
Chandler, Bob, Buff.	60	745	12.4	31	4
Gaines, Clark, N.Y.J.	55	469	8.5	31	1
Moore, Nat, Mia.	52	765	14.7	t73	12
Rashad, Ahmad, Minn.	51	681	13.4	t48	2
McCauley, Don, Balt.	51	495	9.7	t34	2
Scott, James, Chi.	50	809	16.2	t72	3
Swann, Lynn, Pitt.	50	789	15.8	46	7
Pearson, Drew, Dall.	48	870	18.1	67	2
White, Walter, K.C.	48	674	14.0	t48	5

AFC—INDIVIDUALS

	No	Yards	Avg	Long	TDs
Mitchell, Lydell, Balt.	71	620	8.7	38	4
Chandler, Bob, Buff.	60	745	12.4	31	4
Gaines, Clark, N.Y.J.	55	469	8.5	31	1
Moore, Nat, Mia.	52	765	14.7	t73	12
McCauley, Don, Balt.	51	495	9.7	t34	2
Swann, Lynn, Pitt.	50	789	15.8	46	7
White, Walter, K.C.	48	674	14.0	t48	5
Casper, Dave, Oak.	48	584	12.2	27	6
Young, Rickey, S.D.	48	423	8.8	28	0
Stallworth, John, Pitt.	44	784	17.8	49	7
Burrough, Ken, Hou.	43	816	19.0	t85	8
Braxton, Jim, Buff.	43	461	10.7	27	1

	No	Yards	Avg	Long	TDs
Cunningham, Sam, N.E.	42	370	8.8	35	1
Grant, Reuben, Buff.	41	646	15.8	39	2
Miller, Cleo, Clev.	41	291	7.1	28	1

NFC—INDIVIDUALS

	No	Yards	Avg	Long	TDs
Rashad, Ahmad, Minn.	51	681	13.4	t48	2
Scott, James, Chi.	50	809	16.2	t72	3
Pearson, Drew, Dall.	48	870	18.1	67	2
Jackson, Harold, L.A.	48	666	13.9	58	6
Carmichael, Harold, Phil.	46	665	14.5	t50	7
Pearson, Preston, Dall.	46	535	11.6	t36	4
White, Sammy, Minn.	41	760	18.5	t69	9
Galbreath, Tony, N.O.	41	265	6.5	30	0
Harris, Ike, St. L.	40	547	13.7	t38	3
King, Horace, Det.	40	238	6.0	30	0
Jenkins, Alfred, Atl.	39	677	17.4	t73	4
Gray, Mel, St. L.	38	782	20.6	t69	5
Foreman, Chuck, Minn.	38	308	8.1	t31	3
Smith, Barty, G.B.	37	340	9.2	42	1
Fugett, Jean, Wash.	36	631	17.5	52	5

INTERCEPTIONS

INDIVIDUAL CHAMPION
AFC: 10 Lyle Blackwood, Baltimore
NFC: 7 Rolland Lawrence, Atlanta

YARDAGE
AFC: 165 Gary Barbaro, Kansas City
NFC: 157 Bill Simpson, Los Angeles

TOUCHDOWNS
AFC: 1 By fifteen players
NFC: 1 By thirteen players

LONGEST

AFC: 102 Gary Barbaro, Kansas City vs Seattle, December 11 (TD)

NFC: 79 Thomas Henderson, Dallas vs Tampa Bay, October 2 (TD)

Mike Sensibaugh, St. Louis vs New York Giants, October 31 (TD)

TEAM LEADERS

AFC: BALTIMORE 10 Lyle Blackwood; BUFFALO 9 Tony Greene; CINCINNATI 3 Lemar Parrish & Reggie Williams; CLEVELAND 6 Thom Darden; DENVER 5 Billy Thompson; HOUSTON 5 Mike Reinfeldt; KANSAS CITY 8 Gary Barbaro; MIAMI 4 Curtis Johnson; NEW ENGLAND 5 Mike Haynes; NEW YORK JETS 3 Burgess Owens; OAKLAND 6 Jack Tatum; PITTSBURGH 6 Mel Blount; SAN DIEGO 5 Mike Fuller; SEATTLE 6 Autry Beamon

NFC: ATLANTA 7 Rolland Lawrence; CHICAGO 6 Allan Ellis; DALLAS 5 Cliff Harris; DETROIT 6 James Hunter; GREEN BAY 4 Steve Luke & M.C. McCoy; LOS ANGELES 6 Bill Simpson; MINNESOTA 4 Bobby Bryant; NEW ORLEANS 4 Chuck Crist; NEW YORK GIANTS 3 Bill Bryant; PHILADELPHIA 6 Herman Edwards & John Sanders; ST. LOUIS 5 Roger Wehrli; SAN FRANCISCO 2 Mel Phillips & Dave Washington; TAMPA BAY 5 Mike Washington; WASHINGTON 5 Ken Houston

TEAM CHAMPION

AFC: 31 Pittsburgh

NFC: 26 Atlanta

TOP TEN INTERCEPTORS

	No	Yards	Avg	Long	TDs
Blackwood, Lyle, Balt.	10	163	16.3	37	0
Greene, Tony, Buff.	9	144	16.0	47	0
Barbaro, Gary, K.C.	8	165	20.6	t102	1
Clark, Mario, Buff.	7	151	21.6	43	0
Lawrence, Rolland, Atl.	7	138	19.7	36	0
White, Stan, Balt.	7	84	12.0	19	0
Simpson, Bill, L.A.	6	157	26.2	42	0
Tatum, Jack, Oak.	6	146	24.3	41	0
Sanders, John, Phil.	6	122	20.3	45	0
Darden, Thom, Clev.	6	107	17.8	49	1

	No	Yards	Avg	Long	TDs
Blackwood, Lyle, Balt.	10	163	16.3	37	0
Greene, Tony, Buff.	9	144	16.0	47	0
Barbaro, Gary, K.C.	8	165	20.6	t102	1
Clark, Mario, Buff.	7	151	21.6	43	0
White, Stan, Balt.	7	84	12.0	19	0
Tatum, Jack, Oak.	6	146	24.3	41	0
Darden, Thom, Clev.	6	107	17.8	49	1
Blount, Mel, Pitt.	6	65	10.8	37	0
Beamon, Autry, Sea.	6	36	6.0	20	0
Thompson, Billy, Den.	5	122	24.4	38	0
Reinfeldt, Mike, Hou.	5	78	15.6	30	0
Allen, Jim, Pitt.	5	76	15.2	48	0

NFC—INDIVIDUALS

	No	Yards	Avg	Long	TDs
Lawrence, Rolland, Atl.	7	138	19.7	36	0
Simpson, Bill, L.A.	6	157	26.2	42	0
Sanders, John, Phil.	6	122	20.3	45	0
Hunter, James, Det.	6	104	17.3	26	0
Ellis, Allan, Chi.	6	23	3.8	11	0
Edwards, Herman, Phil.	6	9	1.5	6	0
Logan, Randy, Phil.	5	124	24.8	45	0
Thomas, Pat, L.A.	5	97	19.4	30	0
Jackson, Monte, L.A.	5	73	14.6	33	0
Washington, Mike, T.B.	5	71	14.2	t45	1
Houston, Ken, Wash.	5	69	13.8	31	0
Brown, Ray, Atl.	5	56	11.2	24	0

PUNTING

INDIVIDUAL CHAMPION

AFC: 43.3 (Yard Average) Ray Guy, Oakland (59 Punts; 2,552 Yards)

NFC: 42.4 (Yard Average) Tom Blanchard, New Orleans (82 Punts; 3,474 Yards)

NET AVERAGE
AFC: 36.4   Pat McInally, Cincinnati (68 Total Punts; 2,475 Net Yards)
NFC: 35.1   Mike Bragg, Washington (91 Total Punts; 3,194 Net Yards)

LONGEST
AFC: 75 (Yards)   Marv Bateman, Buffalo vs Washington, December 4
NFC: 70 (Yards)   Dave Green, Tampa Bay vs Detroit, November 20

MOST
AFC: 90   Bucky Dilts, Denver (0 Blocked)
NFC: 105   John James, Atlanta (0 Blocked)

TEAM CHAMPION
AFC: 43.3 (Yard Average)   Oakland
NFC: 41.2 (Yard Average)   Atlanta

TOP TEN PUNTERS

	Net Punts	Gross Yards	Long	Gross Avg
Guy, Ray, Oak.	59	2552	74	43.3
Blanchard, Tom, N.O.	82	3474	66	42.4
McInally, Pat, Cin.	67	2802	67	41.8
James, John, Atl.	105	4349	61	41.4
Parsons, Bob, Chi.	80	3232	58	40.4
Green, Dave, T.B.	98	3948	70	40.3
Jennings, Dave, N.Y.G.	100	3993	58	39.9
Beverly, David, G.B.	85	3391	59	39.9
Wilson, Jerrel, K.C.	88	3510	59	39.9
Bateman, Marv, Buff.	81	3229	75	39.9

AFC—INDIVIDUALS

	Net Punts	Gross Yards	Long	Gross Avg
Guy, Ray, Oak.	59	2552	74	43.3
McInally, Pat, Cin.	67	2802	67	41.8

	Net Punts	Gross Yards	Long	Gross Avg
Wilson, Jerrel, K.C.	88	3510	59	39.9
Bateman, Marv, Buff.	81	3229	75	39.9
Weaver, Herman, Sea.	58	2293	59	39.5
Parsley, Cliff, Hou.	77	3030	55	39.4
Dilts, Bucky, Den.	90	3525	63	39.2
Coleman, Greg, Clev.	61	2389	58	39.2
Lee, David, Balt.	82	3142	59	38.3

NFC—INDIVIDUALS

	Net Punts	Gross Yards	Long	Gross Avg
Blanchard, Tom, N.O.	82	3474	66	42.4
James, John, Atl.	105	4349	61	41.4
Parsons, Bob, Chi.	80	3232	58	40.4
Green, Dave, T.B.	98	3948	70	40.3
Jennings, Dave, N.Y.G.	100	3993	58	39.9
Beverly, David, G.B.	85	3391	59	39.9
Clabo, Neil, Minn.	83	3302	69	39.8
White, Danny, Dall.	80	3171	57	39.6

PUNT RETURNS

INDIVIDUAL CHAMPION
AFC: 15.4 (Yard Average)   Billy Johnson, Houston (35 Returns; 539 Yards)
NFC: 10.6 (Yard Average)   Larry Marshall, Philadelphia (46 Returns; 489 Yards)

YARDAGE
AFC: 653   Rick Upchurch, Denver
NFC: 489   Larry Marshall, Philadelphia

RETURNS
AFC: 51   Rick Upchurch, Denver
NFC: 57   Eddie Brown, Washington, NFL record

LONGEST
AFC: 91 (Yards)   Keith Moody, Buffalo vs Cleveland, October 23 (TD)
NFC: 87 (Yards)   Eddie Payton, Detroit vs Minnesota, December 17 (TD)

TOUCHDOWNS
AFC: 6   Billy Johnson, Houston (2) vs Cleveland, October 16 (87 Yards), December 11 (72 Yards)
Mike Fuller, San Diego vs New Orleans, October 9 (88 Yards)
John Kimbrough, Buffalo vs Baltimore, November 13 (73 Yards)
Keith Moody, Buffalo vs Cleveland, October 23 (91 Yards)
Rick Upchurch, Denver vs Pittsburgh, November 6 (87 Yards)
NFC: 4   Bob Hammond, New York Giants vs Dallas, September 25 (68 Yards)
Willard Harrell, Green Bay vs New Orleans, September 18 (75 Yards)
Eddie Payton, Detroit vs Minnesota, December 17 (87 Yards)
Steve Schubert, Chicago vs Detroit, September 18 (70 Yards)

TEAM CHAMPION
AFC: 15.0 (Yard Average)   Houston (36 Returns; 539 Yards)
NFC: 10.4 (Yard Average)   Philadelphia (50 Returns; 518 Yards)

TOP TEN PUNT RETURNERS
	No	FC	Yards	Avg	Long	TDs
Johnson, Billy, Hou.	35	8	539	15.4	t87	2
Morgan, Stanley, N.E.	16	2	220	13.8	53	0
Moody, Keith, Buff.	15	6	196	13.1	t91	1
Fuller, Mike, S.D.	28	2	360	12.9	t88	1
Upchurch, Rick, Den.	51	6	653	12.8	t87	1
Harper, Bruce, N.Y.J.	34	5	425	12.5	49	0
Davis, Tony, Cin.	19	6	220	11.6	70	0
Kimbrough, John, Buff.	16	1	184	11.5	t73	1
Marshall, Larry, Phil.	46	5	489	10.6	48	0
Rodgers, Johnny, S.D.	15	0	158	10.5	52	0

AFC—INDIVIDUALS
	No	FC	Yards	Avg	Long	TDs
Johnson, Billy, Hou.	35	8	539	15.4	t87	2

	No	FC	Yards	Avg	Long	TDs
Morgan, Stanley, N.E.	16	2	220	13.8	53	0
Moody, Keith, Buff.	15	6	196	13.1	t91	1
Fuller, Mike, S.D.	28	2	360	12.9	t88	1
Upchurch, Rick, Den.	51	6	653	12.8	t87	1
Harper, Bruce, N.Y.J.	34	5	425	12.5	49	0
Davis, Tony, Cin.	19	6	220	11.6	70	0
Kimbrough, John, Buff.	16	1	184	11.5	t73	1
Rodgers, Johnny, S.D.	15	0	158	10.5	52	0

NFC—INDIVIDUALS

	No	FC	Yards	Avg	Long	TDs
Marshall, Larry, Phil.	46	5	489	10.6	48	0
Hammond, Bob, N.Y.G.	32	8	334	10.4	t68	1
Payton, Eddie, Clev.-Det.	30	0	290	9.7	t87	1
Schubert, Steve, Chi.	31	9	291	9.4	t70	1
Harrell, Willard, G.B.	28	10	253	9.0	t75	1
Reece, Danny, T.B.	31	2	274	8.8	36	0
Johnson, Butch, Dall.	50	15	423	8.5	38	0
Brown, Eddie, Wash.	57	8	452	7.9	43	0
Metcalf, Terry, St. L.	14	0	108	7.7	23	0
Mauti, Richard, N.O.	37	10	281	7.6	33	0

KICKOFF RETURNS

INDIVIDUAL CHAMPION

AFC: 31.0 (Yard Average)   Raymond Clayborn, New England (28 Returns; 869 Yards)

NFC: 26.9 (Yard Average)   Wilbert Montgomery, Philadelphia (23 Returns; 619 Yards)

YARDAGE

AFC: 1,035   Bruce Harper, New York Jets

NFC: 871   Paul Hofer, San Francisco

RETURNS

AFC: 42   Bruce Harper, New York Jets
NFC: 36   Paul Hofer, San Francisco

LONGEST

AFC: 101 (Yards)   Raymond Clayborn, New England vs
    Baltimore, December 18 (TD)
NFC: 99 (Yards) Wilbert Montgomery, Philadelphia vs
    New York Giants, December 11 (TD)

TOUCHDOWNS

AFC: 5   Raymond Clayborn, New England (3) vs New York Jets,
    October 2 (100 Yards), vs Buffalo, November 6 (93 Yards), vs
    Baltimore, December 18 (101 Yards)
Billy Johnson, Houston vs Chicago, November 6 (76 Yards)
Freddie Solomon, Miami vs Baltimore, October 9 (90 Yards)
NFC: 6   Brian Baschnagel, Chicago vs Atlanta, October 23 (84
    Yards)
Clarence Chapman, New Orleans vs San Francisco, November 27 (92
    Yards)
Terdell Middleton, Green Bay vs Kansas City, November 6 (85 Yards,
    lateral from Steve Odom)
Wilbert Montgomery, Philadelphia vs New York Giants, December 11
    (99 Yards)
Eddie Payton, Detroit vs Minnesota, December 17 (98 Yards)
Dave Williams, San Francisco vs Minnesota, December 4 (80 Yards)

TEAM CHAMPION

AFC: 26.9 (Yard Average)   New England (39 Returns; 1,051
    Yards)
NFC: 24.7 (Yard Average)   Philadelphia (45 Returns; 1,110
    Yards)

TOP TEN KICKOFF RETURNERS

	No	Yards	Avg	Long	TDs
Clayborn, Raymond, N.E.	28	869	31.0	t101	3
Davis, Gary, Mia.	14	414	29.6	73	0
Montgomery, Wilbert, Phil.	23	619	26.9	t99	1
Chapman, Clarence, N.O.	15	385	25.7	t92	1

	No	Yards	Avg	Long	TDs
Johnson, Billy, Hou.	25	630	25.2	t76	1
Brown, Eddie, Wash.	34	852	25.1	46	0
Payton, Eddie, Clev.-Det.	22	548	24.9	t98	1
Harper, Bruce, N.Y.J.	42	1035	24.6	60	0
Johnson, Butch, Dall.	22	536	24.4	64	0
Baschnagel, Brian, Chi.	23	557	24.2	t84	1

AFC—INDIVIDUALS

	No	Yards	Avg	Long	TDs
Clayborn, Raymond, N.E.	28	869	31.0	t101	3
Davis, Gary, Mia.	14	414	29.6	73	0
Johnson, Billy, Hou.	25	630	25.2	t76	1
Harper, Bruce, N.Y.J.	42	1035	24.6	60	0
Smith, Jim, Pitt.	16	381	23.8	37	0
Kimbrough, John, Buff.	15	346	23.1	27	0
Smith, Laverne, Pitt.	16	365	22.8	33	0
Upchurch, Rick, Den.	20	456	22.8	32	0
Hunter, Al, Sea.	36	820	22.8	41	0
Laird, Bruce, Balt.	24	541	22.5	35	0
Shelby, Willie, Cin.	19	403	21.2	38	0
Moody, Keith, Buff.	30	636	21.2	45	0

NFC—INDIVIDUALS

	No	Yards	Avg	Long	TDs
Montgomery, Wilbert, Phil.	23	619	26.9	t99	1
Chapman, Clarence, N.O.	15	385	25.7	t92	1
Brown, Eddie, Wash.	34	852	25.1	46	0
Payton, Eddie, Clev.-Det.	22	548	24.9	t98	1
Johnson, Butch, Dall.	22	536	24.4	64	0
Baschnagel, Brian, Chi.	23	557	24.2	t84	1
Hofer, Paul, S.F.	36	871	24.2	48	0
Metcalf, Terry, St. L.	32	772	24.1	51	0
Brinson, Larry, Dall.	17	409	24.1	41	0
Kane, Rick, Det.	16	376	23.5	33	0
Hagins, Isaac, T.B.	21	493	23.5	41	0
Marshall, Larry, Phil.	20	455	22.8	44	0